CONTENTS

GRAB THESE! 4

GETTING STARTED 6

8
RHINOCEROS BEETLE

10
SCORPION

12
PRAYING MANTIS

14
RED ANT

16
BUTTERFLY

18
TARANTULA

20
COCKROACH

22
HORNET

24
CENTIPEDE

26
HUMMINGBIRD HAWKMOTH

29
LOCUST

GLOSSARY, FURTHER READING, WEBSITES AND INDEX 32

GRAB THESE!

Are you ready to create some amazing pictures? Wait a minute! Before you begin drawing, you will need a few important pieces of equipment.

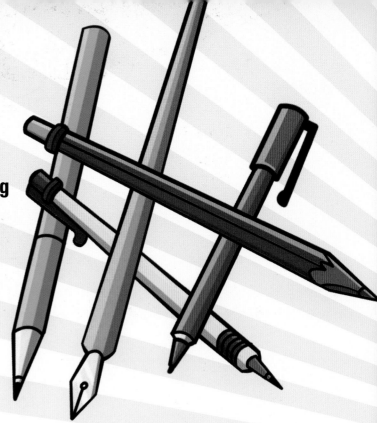

PENS AND PENCILS

You can use a variety of drawing tools including pens, chalks, pencils and paints. But to begin with use an ordinary HB pencil.

PAPER

Use a clean sheet of paper for your final drawings. Scrap paper is useful and cheap for your practice work.

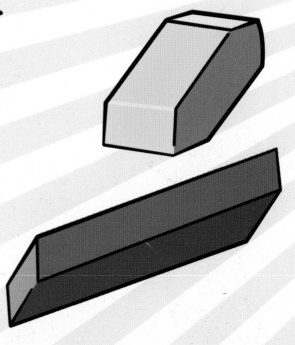

ERASERS

Everyone makes mistakes! That's why every artist has a good eraser. When you rub out a mistake, do it gently. Scrubbing hard at your paper will ruin your drawing and possibly even rip it.

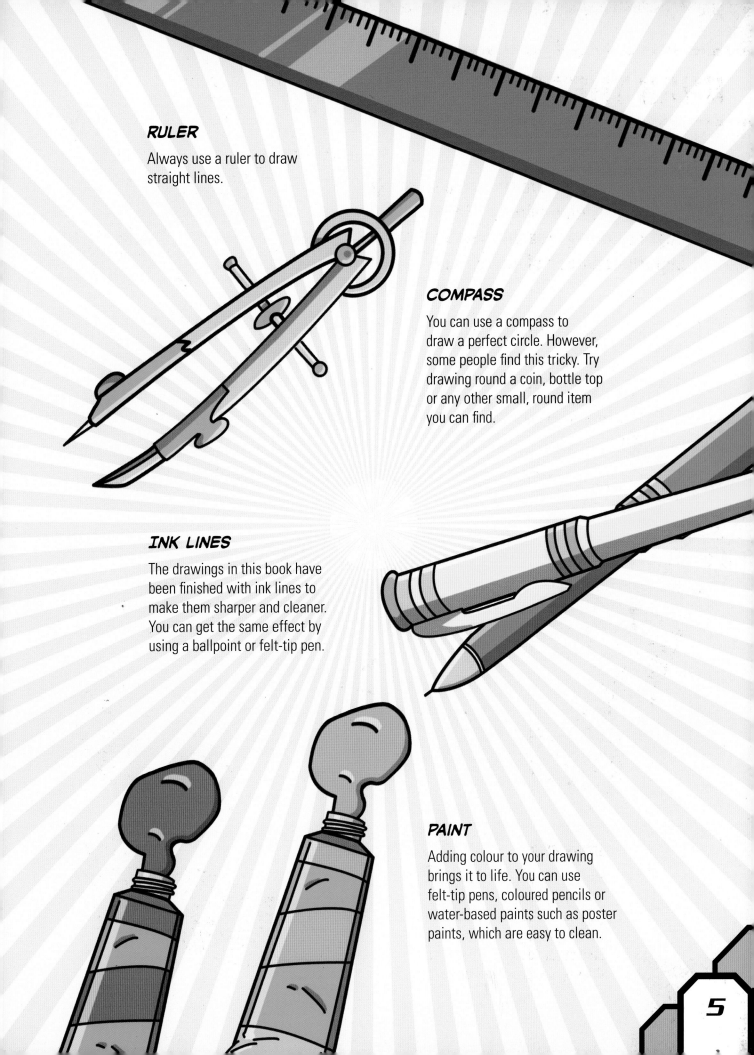

RULER

Always use a ruler to draw straight lines.

COMPASS

You can use a compass to draw a perfect circle. However, some people find this tricky. Try drawing round a coin, bottle top or any other small, round item you can find.

INK LINES

The drawings in this book have been finished with ink lines to make them sharper and cleaner. You can get the same effect by using a ballpoint or felt-tip pen.

PAINT

Adding colour to your drawing brings it to life. You can use felt-tip pens, coloured pencils or water-based paints such as poster paints, which are easy to clean.

GETTING STARTED

In this book we use a simple two-colour system to show you how to draw a picture. Just remember: new lines are blue lines!

STARTING WITH STEP 1

The first lines you will draw are very simple shapes. They will be shown in blue, like this. You should draw them with a normal HB pencil.

ADDING MORE DETAIL

As you move on to the next step, the lines you have already drawn will be shown in black. The new lines for that stage will appear in blue.

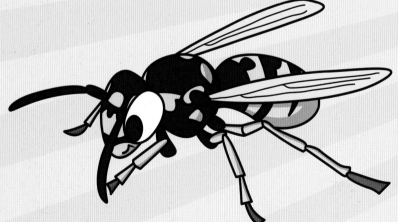

FINISHING YOUR PICTURE

When you reach the final stage you will see the image in full colour with a black ink line. Inking a picture means tracing the main lines with a black pen. After the ink dries, use your eraser to remove all the pencil lines before adding your colour.

ADDING MOVEMENT

Here are some fun ways to make your bugs look as though they're really moving. Follow these tips and pretty soon they'll be crawling or buzzing off your page.

FLOATY MOVEMENT

Show how a butterfly flutters through the air by adding a small, dotted line that traces the path it has flown.

SPEED LINES

Bugs such as cockroaches move quickly, but this can be difficult to show on paper. Add simple lines coming away from the the bug's back end. Draw a puff of smoke and it will really zoom along.

VIBRATION LINES

You can easily make the wings of your bug look as though they are moving back and forth. Just add simple vibration lines that follow the line of the edges of the wings, as shown here.

SNAP, SNAP!

A sudden movement, such as a fierce snap from a claw, can be shown by adding a cartoon flash. This spiky shape will give your drawing some extra drama. Look out!

RHINOCEROS BEETLE

The rhinoceros beetle is a large insect with two huge horns on its head, which it uses for fighting and digging. It also has very thick and shiny 'armour'.

STEP 1

First, draw the horns. Follow the shape on the right and then add a long oval for the beetle's body.

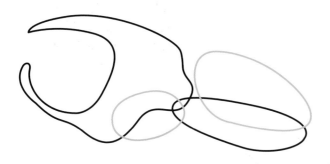

STEP 2

Next, add two oval shapes to create the beetle's wing cover and face.

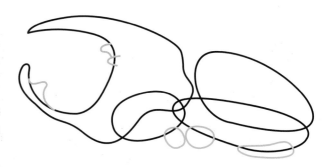

STEP 3

Draw some fine details on the horns and add three oval shapes to begin the beetle's legs.

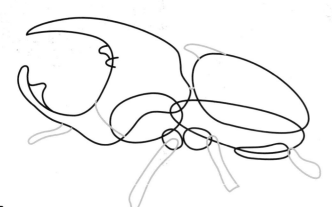

STEP 4

Add the legs and the spike on the beetle's body. Then add a curved line across the horns.

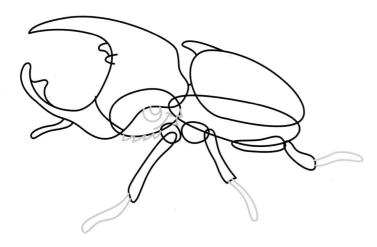

STEP 5

Finally, add the last part of the legs and complete the outline of the head as shown. Then add its eye.

STEP 6

A rhinoceros beetle may look fierce but it's actually harmless. To make its body look super shiny, add a white line across its back as shown below.

SCORPION

A scorpion is part of the spider family. It has eight legs and a huge pair of claws. Its long, thin tail curves over its back… and there is a nasty sting at the end of it!

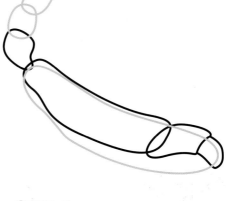

STEP 1

Begin to draw the scorpion's body by linking together these four shapes.

STEP 2

Draw over the first outline with these three shapes. The two small ovals mark the start of its famous tail.

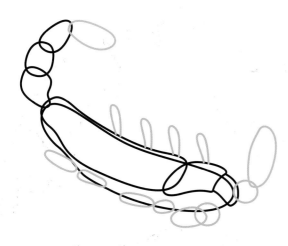

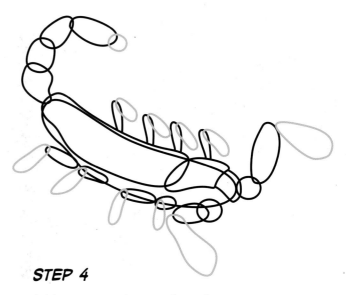

STEP 3

These small loops are the start of the legs. There are four on each side and two for each of the claws at the front. Add another oval to the tail.

STEP 4

Add some more loops to form the next segments of the legs, claws and tail. A 'segment' is part of an insect's body.

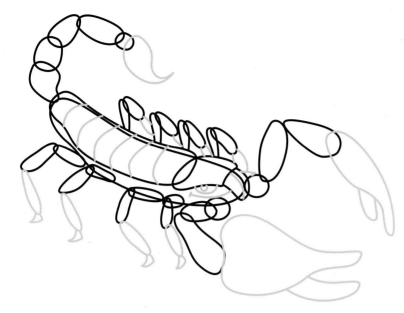

STEP 5

Draw the last segments of the legs and add six stripy lines across the main body. Then, add the large, snappy claws and the sharp sting in the tail. Lastly, draw the scorpion's face.

STEP 6

Colour your scorpion red. It may have a smiling face, but don't be fooled. The sneaky glint in its eye suggests that it may be about to strike!

PRAYING MANTIS

A praying mantis is a rather strange insect! It has a triangular head, a long body and large front legs. The front legs are folded in a way that makes the bug look like it's praying.

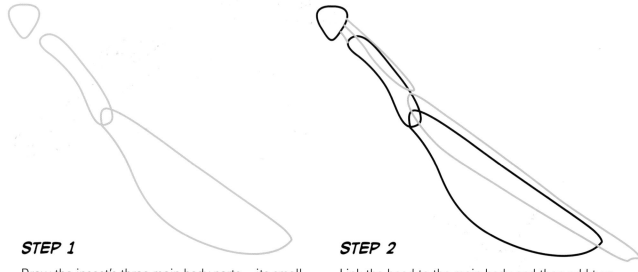

STEP 1

Draw the insect's three main body parts – its small, triangular head and two longer shapes.

STEP 2

Link the head to the main body and then add two narrow shapes to form its wings.

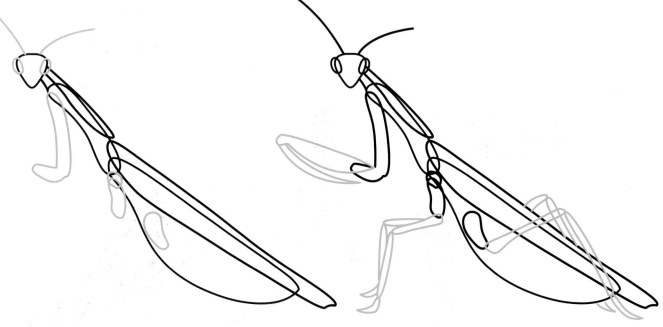

STEP 3

Now, add its eyes and long antennae. Three small shapes begin the middle and back legs and a shape like the letter 'J' is the start of its front legs.

STEP 4

Next, add the insect's long, thin back legs and its bent middle legs. Finish off the large front legs.

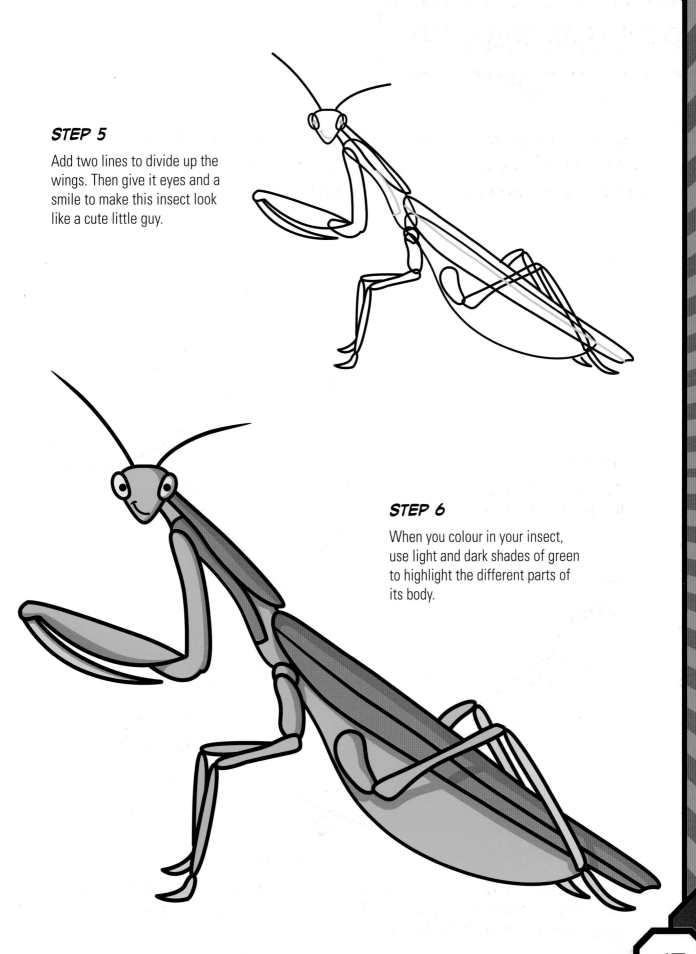

STEP 5

Add two lines to divide up the wings. Then give it eyes and a smile to make this insect look like a cute little guy.

STEP 6

When you colour in your insect, use light and dark shades of green to highlight the different parts of its body.

RED ANT

Red ants are sometimes known as fire ants because of their reddish colour. These tiny but fierce insects live in large groups called colonies. Like all insects, they have six legs.

STEP 1

First, make up the ant's body from these bean-like shapes. Make sure the head is slightly flattened.

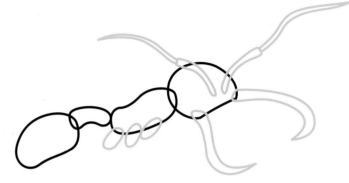

STEP 2

Next, add two sharp pincers and long antennae. Draw three ovals for the start of the leg joints.

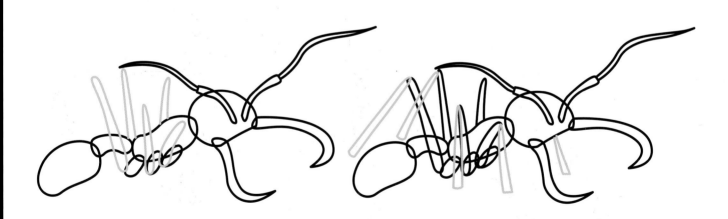

STEP 3

Add long segments to the ant's skinny legs, as shown here.

STEP 4

Add another set of segments to the legs, so they point downwards.

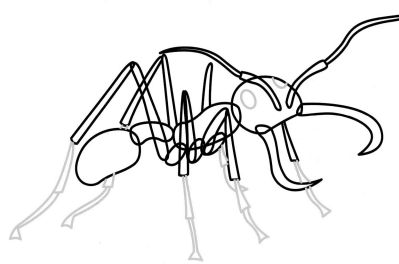

STEP 5

Draw the final segments of the ant's six legs and add a pair of eyes.

STEP 6

Red ants spend most of their time on the forest floor. Colour them with reddish-brown colours to keep them hidden!

BUTTERFLY

Butterflies come in many different colours and patterns. This one is yellow and orange… but you could choose any colours you like.

STEP 1

First, draw a small, round head, a sausage shape for the body and two antennae.

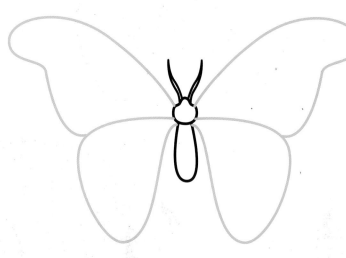

STEP 2

Draw the butterfly's large and beautiful wings next. Try to make the two wings exactly the same shape.

STEP 3

Add some markings to the wings. Then draw some stripy lines on the insect's body.

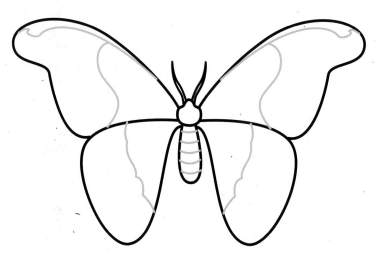

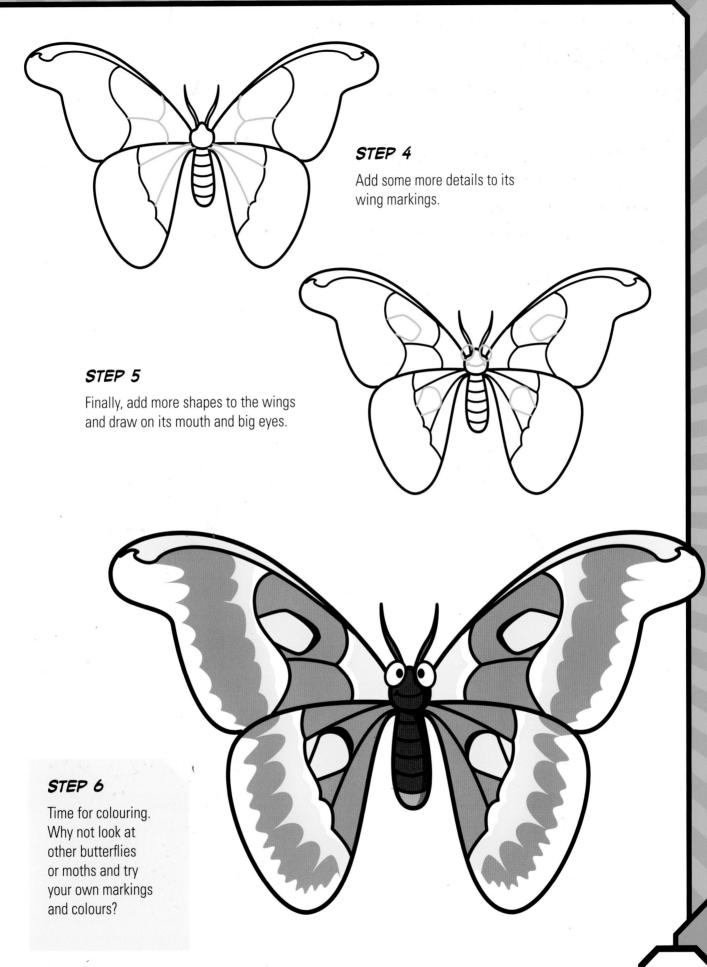

STEP 4

Add some more details to its wing markings.

STEP 5

Finally, add more shapes to the wings and draw on its mouth and big eyes.

STEP 6

Time for colouring. Why not look at other butterflies or moths and try your own markings and colours?

TARANTULA

A tarantula is a big spider with a large, hairy body. It has eight stripy legs, which are covered in tiny hairs. It hunts for food at night, catching insects and even small reptiles.

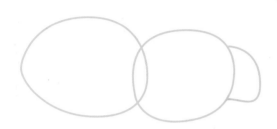

STEP 1

First, draw two overlapping oval shapes to make the body and head. Add a smaller shape to make the mouth at the front.

STEP 2

Next, draw four ovals and five sausage shapes to begin to form the spider's eight legs and one of its feelers.

STEP 3

Now, add some more segments to the spider's long, thin legs and its feeler.

STEP 4

Next, add more oval-shaped leg segments and the outline of the other feeler.

STEP 5

Complete the legs, then add curved zigzags along the outline of its head and body to make it furry. Add large eyes and a line down the spider's mouth.

SUPER TIP!

Tarantulas are covered in tiny hairs that give them a slightly furry appearance.

- Draw the main body shape and colour it in.

- Then add short lines dotted around. Only use a few to make it slightly furry, rather than completely hairy like a bear!

STEP 6

We've coloured our spider using black and orange. Each segment of the legs is a different colour, to make a stripy pattern.

COCKROACH

A cockroach is a tough little insect that has lived since the time of the dinosaurs! This six-legged bug can skitter along very quickly. It likes to hide in dark corners.

STEP 1

First, draw these three shapes to make the insect's body and head.

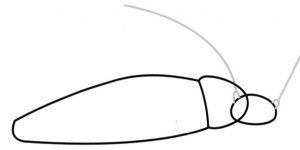

STEP 2

Next, add some very long antennae to the cockroach's head.

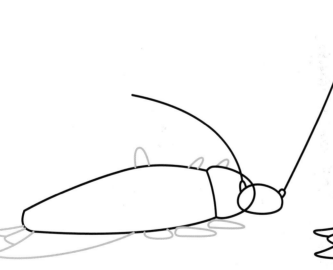

STEP 3

Draw three shapes at the back to make the folded wings and add six ovals to start the legs.

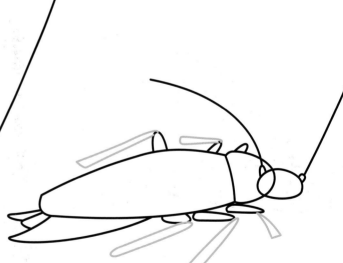

STEP 4

Now add five longer shapes to five of the ovals to give the insect proper legs.

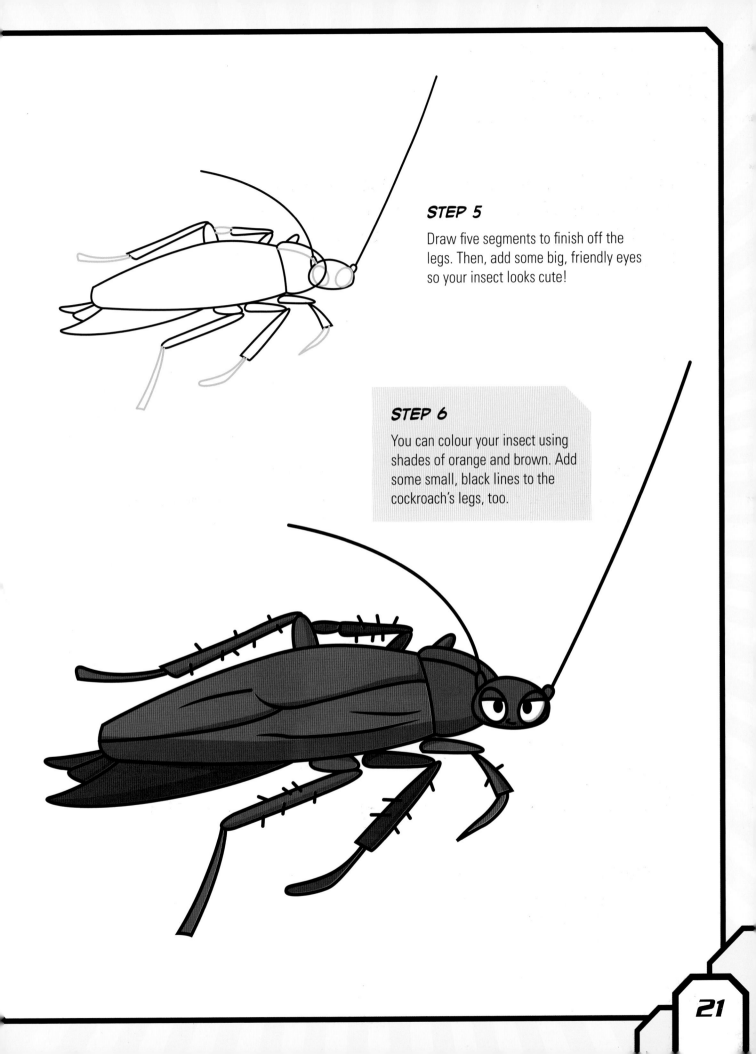

STEP 5

Draw five segments to finish off the legs. Then, add some big, friendly eyes so your insect looks cute!

STEP 6

You can colour your insect using shades of orange and brown. Add some small, black lines to the cockroach's legs, too.

HORNET

A hornet looks a bit like a wasp, only bigger. It has a smooth body, long wings and bold, black and yellow markings. But beware, this insect can give you a nasty sting!

STEP 1

First, draw three oval shapes to make the hornet's head and body.

STEP 2

Next, add the long antennae and eye. Draw a small circle on the middle part of the hornet. This is where the wing joins on.

STEP 3

Next come the long and very thin wings. Add three ovals to begin its legs.

STEP 4

Add more segments to create the hornet's long legs.

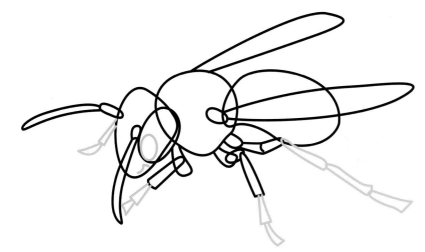

STEP 5

Finish the legs as shown above. Add a pupil to the insect's eye and a little smiling mouth.

SUPER TIP!

- To create see-through wings for bugs such as hornets, wasps and bees, first draw vein lines.

- Colour the wings in a very light shade. Pale blue works best.

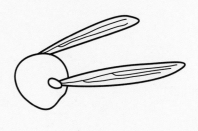

STEP 6

Yellow and black warn you to keep your distance from this super-sized stinger!

CENTIPEDE

The name centipede may mean '100 legs' but this bug actually has around 40. Its long body is made up of lots of segments. Each segment has its own pair of legs.

STEP 1

First, draw a long curved line. You can make it any shape you want as long as you keep it slightly curved.

STEP 2

Starting at the back of your centipede, draw a very small egg shape. Move along the line drawing the same shape again and again. Make each one slightly larger as you go.

STEP 3

Draw a small, curved line where each circle joins to start the legs.

STEP 4

Now you have made a start on all the legs, go over them again and thicken them up.

STEP 5

Add the centipede's tail and antennae. Don't forget some nice, big eyes so your centipede can see where it's going.

STEP 6

Add a darker shade to the bottom edge of the circles when you're colouring. This will give the body a nice, rounded shape.

SUPER TIP!

We've drawn our centipede in a straight line to show you how to do it, but you can pose yours any way you want to.

- Sketch your first line in any shape you want. Here, we've drawn a more curved line.

- Then, start building your circle shapes along the line like this.

HUMMINGBIRD HAWKMOTH

This moth is sometimes mistaken for a bird! Its wings beat so fast that they make a humming sound as the moth hovers over flowers. Its long proboscis (the part that looks like a nose) dips into flowers and collects nectar.

STEP 1

First, draw a shape like this to give you the moth's body outline.

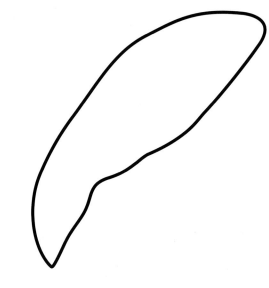

STEP 2

Add a large, flat wing to help your moth hover like a hummingbird. Add a pair of antennae and an oval shape for its leg.

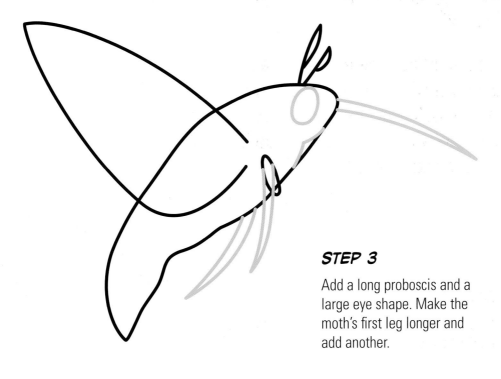

STEP 3

Add a long proboscis and a large eye shape. Make the moth's first leg longer and add another.

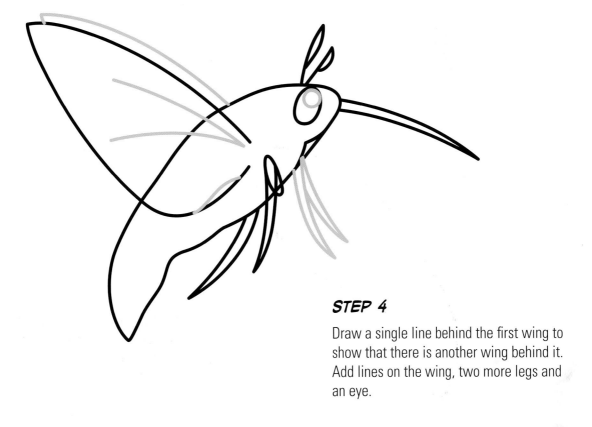

STEP 4

Draw a single line behind the first wing to show that there is another wing behind it. Add lines on the wing, two more legs and an eye.

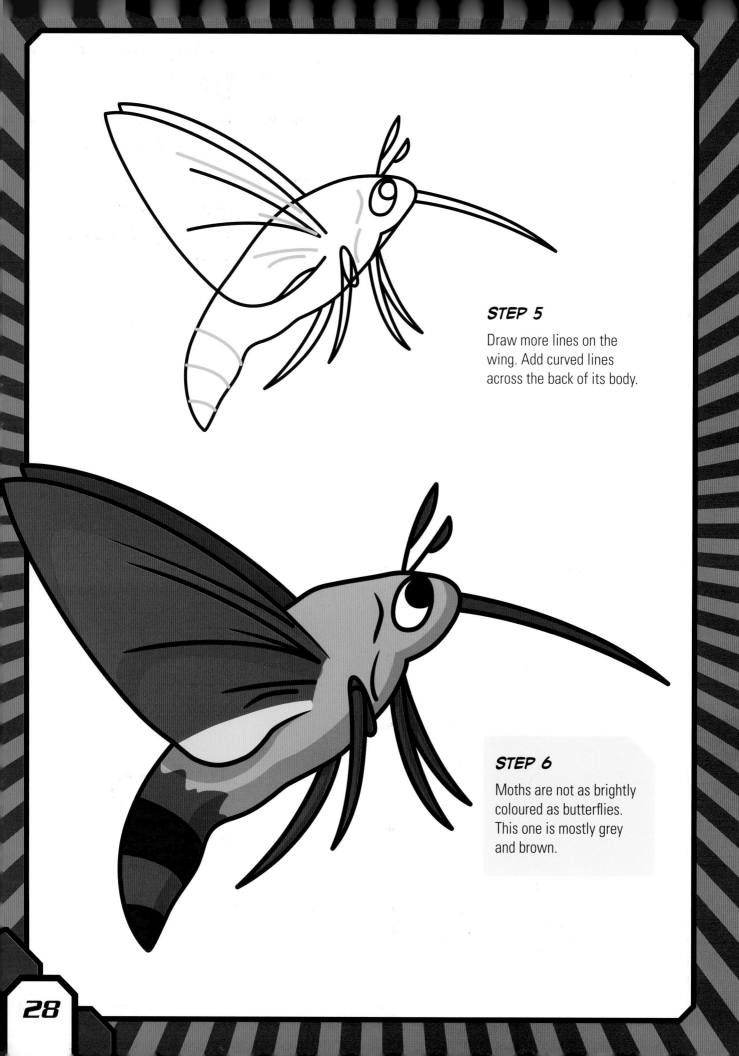

STEP 5

Draw more lines on the wing. Add curved lines across the back of its body.

STEP 6

Moths are not as brightly coloured as butterflies. This one is mostly grey and brown.

A locust is an insect that belongs to the grasshopper family. It has long, powerful back legs that help it to leap through the air. It also has wings, so it can fly!

STEP 1

First, draw a long, curving body that leads up to a chunky neck. Add a teardrop-shaped head.

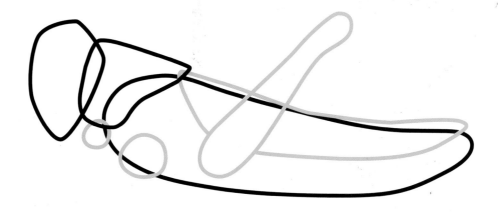

STEP 2

Next, add a wing case and the start of a long back leg. Then draw two ovals. They will turn into the two front legs.

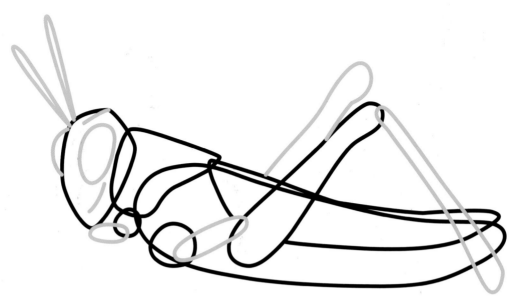

STEP 3

Draw a pair of short antennae. Add big eyes, an eyebrow and a mouth. Draw more leg segments. Its long legs will help it to hop!

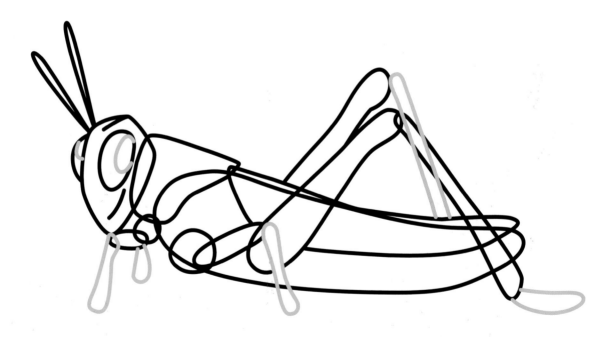

STEP 4

Finish the strong back legs and add more segments to the other legs and detail to the eyes.

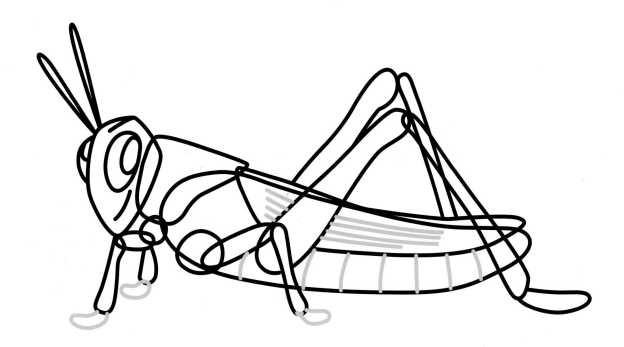

STEP 5

Draw the feet, and add some lines on the wing case and lower body.

STEP 6

Choose some different shades of yellow and orange for your locust. Now it's ready to hop off the page!

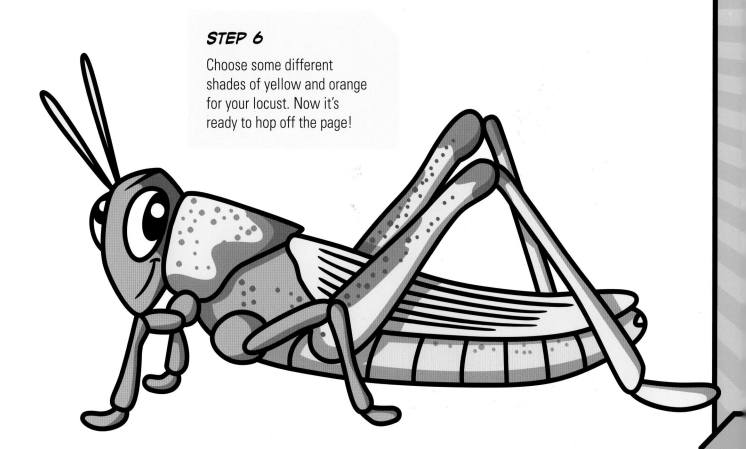

GLOSSARY

antennae Long, thin organs on the head of an insect that are used to touch and feel things.

colony A group of insects.

feeler A movable part on an insect used for touching things.

HB pencil A pencil that is neither soft not hard, but something in between.

nectar A sweet liquid produced by flowering plants.

pincer A claw.

proboscis A long, thin tube that forms part of the mouth of some insects.

pupil The dark centre part of the eye.

reptile An animal such as a snake or a lizard.

segment Part of an insect's body.

vein A thin line on the wing of an insect.

wing case A hard covering over the wings of an insect.

FURTHER READING

How to Draw Brilliant Bugs by Lisa Regan (Miles Kelly Publishing, 2011)

How to Draw Insects in Simple Steps by Dandi Palmer (Search Press, 2013)

What to Doodle? Creepy Crawlies! by Chuck Whelon (Dover Children's, 2011)

WEBSITES

animals.nationalgeographic.co.uk/animals/bugs/

www.dltk-kids.com/Crafts/insects/

www.dragoart.com/insects-c174-1.htm

INDEX

ants 14–15
bees 23
beetles 8–9
butterflies 7, 16–17, 28
centipedes 24–25
claws 7, 10, 11
cockroaches 7, 20–21
colours 5, 6, 11, 13, 14, 15, 16, 17, 19, 21, 23, 25, 28

erasers 4, 6
hornets 22–23
locusts 29–31
moths 17, 26–28
movement 7
paints 4, 5
paper 4
pencils 4, 6
pens 4, 5, 6

praying mantises 12–13
rulers 5
scorpions 10–11
spiders 10, 18–19
stings 10, 11, 22, 23
tarantulas 18–19
wasps 22, 23
wings 7, 12, 13, 16, 17, 20, 22, 23, 26, 27, 29